The

Jesse Duplantis

JDM Publications

The Sovereignty of God
ISBN 978-09743829-6-8
Copyright ©2005 Jesse Duplantis
Published by Jesse Duplantis Ministries

2nd Printing 2010
Jesse Duplantis Ministries
PO Box 1089
Destrehan, Louisiana 70047
USA
www.jdm.org

Jesse Duplantis Ministries is dedicated to reaching people and changing lives with the Gospel of Jesus Christ. For more information, or to purchase other products from Jesse Duplantis Ministries, please contact us at the address above.

Introduction

When bad things happen and people don't know what to say, there is a word that inevitably comes up to explain the problem away. It is sovereignty.

Sovereignty is a theological term which refers to God's right and power to do whatever He wants to do. When healing doesn't manifest or when babies die and hurricanes blow houses away, Christians will often site "the sovereignty of God" as the reason for the tragedy. "He's God," they say. "He's sovereign and can do whatever He wants to do." That sounds good enough, doesn't it? But, there is a real problem with this kind of thinking.

You see, if you believe that God doesn't keep His Word and that He will break His promises, then sovereignty as a reason for tragedy makes real sense. But, if you believe that God is righteous and just, that He will honor His Word

3

and His promises to you, then this kind of reasoning falls to pieces with even the smallest amount of scripture. The Bible itself is filled with promises and stories of how God honors His Word.

God *is* sovereign and has unlimited power, no doubt about it. Yet, He has chosen to limit Himself to what He will and will not do concerning mankind, and He spelled it out in His Word. This makes Him sovereign, *outside* of His Word.

Can God do anything? Yes. Will God do anything? No. God has already said what He'll do in many situations in the Holy Bible. God has chosen to bind Himself with His own Word, and that's what makes Him so worthy of our trust.

God promises, *"My covenant will I not break, nor alter the thing that is gone out of My lips"* (Psalm 89:34). We know that He can't lie, and we know the father of all lies is the devil (See Titus 1:2; John 8:44). Yet, people still talk about God as if He breaks promises on a whim. This is not true.

God is a promise-keeper, not a promise-breaker. I'm going to share some truth with you about

God and His unchanging Word on healing, the story of Job, God's wrath, and babies that die too young. My hope is that you will come away with a greater understanding of the faithfulness of your Father, God.

Chapter 1
Does Everything Good and Bad Come from God?

Traditional thinking says that everything good comes from God and everything bad comes from God. But, if that's true, what is the devil doing? Twiddling his thumbs in hell?

Many people have ignorantly blamed God for killing babies, sending sickness and withholding healing from believers, instead of holding the true culprit responsible for killing, stealing, and destroying lives.

Even in the Old Testament, it is clear that most people were in the dark about God. They thought that God did everything good as well as everything bad. They really didn't have a revelation of the devil and his works.

In the New Testament, Jesus came on the scene to let us know the truth about God *and* the devil.

We needed somebody to come down here and wipe out our sin so we could see clearly and really know God on a personal level. That someone who did this for us was Jesus Christ, the Son of God. Jesus redeemed man from sin and gave us victory over satan. Jesus washed away the sin-barrier between God and man with His shed blood (Matt. 26:28; 1 John 1:7; Heb. 9:14; Eph. 1:7, 2:13; Col. 1:20).

Yet, before Jesus ever went to the cross, He taught us some valuable lessons about life's ups and downs. Jesus revealed more about the devil than was previously known through His teachings and His life examples. He was revolutionary in every way.

Jesus was the first to shine a bright light on the devil's work within the earth. He said, *"The thief cometh not, but for to steal, and to kill, and to destroy: I am come that they might have life, and that they might have it more abundantly. I am the Good Shepherd: the Good Shepherd giveth His life for the sheep"* (John 10:10-11).

Jesus exposed the devil. It was as if He was saying, and I'm paraphrasing here: 'There's a devil roaming the earth. He's trying to kill you, steal from you, and destroy you. He's bad and wants to take your life. But I am good and I want to give you a good life. I want to guide you and nourish you like a Good Shepherd. In fact, I love you so much that I'm going to die for you.'

Jesus Exposed Demons

When Jesus came on the scene, He didn't watch idly as satan tormented and afflicted people. He did something about it. He had compassion on the people. He spoke truth. He went around doing good deeds. He also did miracles. He healed, He raised the dead. He delivered all that were oppressed by the devil.

"How God anointed Jesus of Nazareth with the Holy Ghost and with power: Who went about doing good, and healing all that were oppressed of the devil; for God was with Him" (Acts 10:38).

Do you ever read of Jesus putting sickness on someone? Do you ever read of Him oppressing anyone or hurting anyone? If Jesus didn't do it in His life, what makes you think that He'll do it now? After all, isn't it good to heal? Isn't it good to save? Isn't it good to help others?

Ask yourself, if healing were not from God, would Jesus have done it? If deliverance was not from God, would Jesus have freed so many?

Jesus was good, and He served a good Father. He knew people would have a hard time believing that He was the Son of God, so He said,

"Believest thou not that I am in the Father, and the Father in Me? the words that I speak unto you I speak not of Myself: but the Father that dwelleth in Me, He doeth the works. Believe Me that I am in the Father, and the Father in Me: or else believe Me for the very works' sake" (John 14:10-11).

In other words, Jesus wants us to believe that He is completely linked to His Father, in Word and in will. Jesus also wants us to look at His works. They are a clue about Who He was when He was here on earth and what He was here for. They also give us insight into what He means to do for us today.

Jesus always spoke well of His Father, and when it was needed, He put the devil and his demons in their place – under His feet! At one point, demons actually spoke up to Jesus and said, *"...What have we to do with Thee, Jesus, Thou Son of God? Art Thou come hither to torment us before the time?"* (Matt. 8:29).

Isn't that something?! The demons thought *they* were being tormented! They were upset because they were finally getting a little payback, Jesus-style! Glory! That makes me want to shout!

Not only did Jesus take authority over the devil

and his works, He also told us that we could do the same. John 14:12 says, *"Verily, verily, I say unto you, He that believeth on Me, the works that I do shall he do also; and greater works than these shall he do; because I go unto My Father."*

Read through the Gospels again and see how much authority Jesus exercised over the devil. He didn't give him one inch! And, He never blamed His Father for anything. He only sought to bring glory to the Father and to put the devil in his place. Through Christ's great example, we can learn how to live in authority too, to rebuke and resist the devil when needed, and to always give the utmost respect to our Father, God.

God Always Keeps His Promises

One time while I was praying, the Lord spoke something to my heart that I believe may help you to understand the way He works. He said, "Jesse, My Word shall not return unto Me void. But it is very possible that My Word can return unto you void."

"What?" I said. "Why, Lord?"

"Because you don't believe it like I do."

That was deep for me and showed me the

importance of my own personal faith. His Word had returned to *me* void, but it never returned to *Him* void. In other words, He never broke His promise to me. He always believed and fulfilled His Word. He always did His part.

But, sometimes, I didn't really believe His Word in faith; sometimes I didn't do my part. So, there were times when I'd stopped my own success in receiving from God either through my lack of knowledge, lack of patience, or lack of faith.

The bottom line is that personal experiences don't prove or disprove God's Word and will. When it comes to His Word, there's no such thing of whether God wants to do something or doesn't want to do it. He will always keep His Word, always. Once God has said something, He will not alter the words that have been spoken.

Promises or covenants are important to God. He said, ***"My covenant will I not break, nor alter the thing that is gone out of My lips"*** (Psalm 89:34). In other words, He has promised to keep His promise!

Some people think that God will break His Word. They think this because maybe someone who was prayed for didn't receive healing, and they died. But, God doesn't use circumstances as a measuring stick for following through with His Word. To do that would mean He was an unfair God.

So, if Isaiah 53:5 says that by the stripes laid on Jesus' back we are healed, that is a promise to us. The fact may be that somebody is sick, but the truth is that Jesus paid the price for healing. If a person doesn't get healed, is it God's fault? Is sovereignty a valid excuse for someone not receiving healing? Many people believe this way.

Will God break His Word? Will He withhold healing through the blood of Jesus because of some special circumstance? No. Regardless of circumstances, He won't break His Word. He has promised to keep His promises.

From the beginning, God has been a promise-keeper. Even in the Old Testament, there are scriptures that show us the loyal nature of God. God often swears by Himself in the Bible, just to show that He means business.

When God was talking to Abraham in Genesis 22:16-17 after the angel stopped him from sacrificing Isaac, God said that He would swear by Himself to keep the covenant because there was no one greater to swear by. He did it again in

Isaiah 45:23, Jeremiah 22:5 and even Amos 4:2.

The truth is that God is sovereign in that He can do what He wants, when He wants, but, again, He has made a choice to bind Himself by His own Word. So, that makes Him sovereign *outside* of what His Holy Word says.

Chapter 2
Sovereignty and Healing

Healing is where sovereignty often gets misused. The truth is that healing is under our covenant with God through Jesus Christ.

So, when someone tells me that the reason someone didn't get healed is because God is sovereign and His will was death, I think only one thing. *Either you're lying or God's lying. And, I pick you.*

God made a promise when Jesus was getting His back beaten with a whip. He was making a covenant with mankind that day, and He has yet to say it's "not for today."

When we're talking about healing, the word "sovereignty" shouldn't even come into the conversation. Why? Because healing is a promise in the Word. God said it, and He meant it. When we say "God is sovereign" as a reason for a person not getting healed, we're calling God a liar. We're saying He broke His Word.

If you lay hands on the sick, and they don't recover and they end up dying, it's not God's fault. We sometimes want it to be His fault because we don't understand why they died, but that doesn't make it right to accuse God of anything.

People use the sovereignty excuse when sick believers die because they don't know what else to say. They want to be compassionate. They want to offer solace. People want answers.

When there are no easy answers, preachers sometimes blame God by saying, "He's sovereign. Sometimes we have to accept that healing wasn't God's will." This lets everybody off the hook – except God. He just got accused of killing somebody, for withholding the healing blood of Jesus and for going back on His Word. It's a slap in the face to our good God.

Reasons that Christians Die Sick

There are a lot of reasons why people can die even after they've prayed for healing – too many to mention in this little book.

Sometimes, they don't really believe in healing. They might profess it with their mouth because they think it's the right thing to do, but inside, they feel that sickness, disease and eventually, death, is just part of life.

Other times, they secretly want to escape this life. You'd be surprised how many people claim they want healing and secretly just want to go home to Heaven. They've already given up in their heart. They're tired of fighting their body and the devil – they've become weary in well-doing. They simply don't want to do it anymore.

Other times, there is a huge amount of fear present, and it just cancels out the force of faith. You'd be surprised how many people claim they're standing on the Word, but live in fear of death the whole time they're laying in the hospital bed. They ball and squall one minute in fear and then, pull themselves up and claim strong faith when a fellow Christian walks through the door. That's like trying to drive cross-country and stopping every fifteen minutes for a coffee break. You won't get anywhere soon.

Also, you'd be surprised how often *other* people hinder the healing process. Many times, Christians will come to pray and lay hands on the sick, but when they leave the hospital room, they immediately stop believing. They just prayed a great prayer – of doubt – and they don't believe that the person will be healed any more than they believe that the moon is made of cheese. They came to just give it their best shot with God. That's what I call gambling at the Gospel casino. Their faith is cracking before they hit the door, and that's no good for the sick person!

Other times, a person has no foundation in the love and mercy of God. They wonder still if He loves them enough to heal them. They may have a lot of issues surrounding worthiness and so, they feel that they can't boldly approach the throne of grace in their time of need. They may pray, but they cannot release full faith in God because they aren't really sure that He'll come through, which means that they aren't sure God loves them.

There are so many other situations surrounding the death of sick Christians, none of which have anything to do with the sovereign power of God. Do a study for yourself in the scripture on those that were healed under Jesus' ministry. Notice the desperate "must have it" type of faith that some had. Notice the single-minded focus on the healing power of God.

Yet, you will also see in researching the scriptures that there was also a time when Jesus could not heal anyone. Was it because He didn't have the power? No, it is because He was dealing with a group of people who didn't believe that He was Who He said He was. They were unsure of Him as God's Son. Surety is a critical part in receiving healing.

The Spirit, Mind and Body
Work Together

It's important to establish strong faith for healing before sickness ever arises because it's much harder to play "catch up" in your faith when your body is physically weak.

The body responds to the mind and the spirit. But, if the mind is arguing with the spirit, what do you think the body will do? Nothing, it will keep on doing its own thing until a stronger voice tells it what to do. The body is just a vessel for the real you, the combination of your recreated spirit and your soul, which is your mind, will, and emotions.

Walking in love towards others is also a critical part of receiving healing. After all, how can we expect our faith to work when we're not walking in love? Galatians 5:6 tells us that faith actually *works* by love. If we're in unforgiveness towards another person or sowing seeds of discord, that stops our faith from working. Faith is crucial to receiving healing power; so love must also be paramount in our lives.

Your spirit is strong, but your mind needs conditioning – transforming – and the way to do that is to saturate yourself with the Word of God. Let it renew your mind so that you believe it, because that's when you're going to receive it in your body. Your body will listen to what your mind is saying, so line up your mind with the Word.

Who Knows the Heart of Man?

When I hear someone say that God is sovereign in regards to healing, I just want to shout, "Tell the truth! You just don't know why they didn't get healed!" Sometimes people don't have a clue why and are just grasping for straws. Preachers are bad about not wanting to admit that they don't know why a manifestation of healing did not happen.

Sometimes things happen that are hard to explain when looking at the surface of events. Who can know the heart of another person? Who can measure the faith of all those involved?

Who would admit to not believing while they're slapping anointing oil on a dying person? Those kinds of heart-issues are only known to God.

Some situations are obvious and we can say, "This seems like the reason." But the truth is that, unless we ask God for wisdom and understanding and receive that from Him, there are some things in life that we may not know or understand until we get to Heaven.

The Power is Present
Spirit, Soul and Body

"But I don't think God heals everybody, Brother Jesse." Really? Then, I guess He doesn't save everybody who wants salvation either. That cross-thing had some sure bets and some not-so-sure bets, right? Wrong. The truth is that salvation is always present. But it isn't always received... just like healing and everything else Jesus died to give us.

In Luke 5:17, it says that the doctors and the Pharisees of the Law were sitting nearby and Jesus was teaching. There was the one that was sick of the palsy and the Bible says the power of the Lord was present to heal them. To heal who?

Not the sick of the palsy guy. He hadn't even gotten there yet. The power was present to heal the Pharisee and the doctor of the law, but they didn't receive it. So, consequently, the man who was sick received it all. The healing power was present, but the Pharisees couldn't receive the power from Jesus.

When Jesus told the sick man to pick up his bed and walk because his sins were forgiven, it shook the Pharisees up. Yet, Jesus was showing us that He deals with the heart *before* the body. The heart is what is changed first, then the mind and the body. The heart accepts healing first, then, the mind and the body.

Do you know that salvation has already been planned and made available to everyone on the planet? Yet, it is up to each of us to accept it. Jesus died for the sins of the past, the present, and the future. His blood that was shed on the cross has provided redemption for all that call upon Him – our answer was given before we ever had a problem.

What people have to do is believe in their heart and confess with their mouth that Jesus rose from the dead and then, they are saved. First, it happens in the heart. Then, the soul receives the salvation. People who are going to Hell are going for rejecting Jesus' sacrifice. That is a fact. The Lord has already done the work. Why can't we just accept what He has already done?

We've got to believe in our heart and confess with our mouth if we want salvation (Romans 10:9-10). The same is true with all the rest that Jesus died to give us. We can't just believe in our heart that He *can* save or heal us, but we have to believe that He *will*. Is it His will? Yes.

God's Word is His will.

Chapter 3
What Is A Sovereign Act of God?

So, what exactly *is* a sovereign act of God? The perfect example is the story of Saul of Tarsus on the road to Damascus. This incident had nothing to do with God's already established Word. In this story, God decided to do something to get Saul's attention. (Turn to Acts, chapter nine, for the full story.)

Now, think about what's going on here. Saul is angry. He's so angry that he has decided to kill some Christians. The Bible says he's so ticked off that he's *"...breathing out threatenings and slaughter against the disciples of the Lord..."* (Acts 9:1).

This man is mad, and he's looking to hurt somebody. He's in pure rage. The Lord decides to sovereignly intervene. God slaps him off his donkey, shines a light around him, and starts talking to Saul. I'll paraphrase, 'Why are you persecuting Me, Saul?' Saul is blown away by this and says, 'Who are you, Lord?'

'I'm Jesus, the One you're persecuting!'

'OK, Lord. What do You want me to do?'

God tells him to go to the city and he'll be told what to do when he gets there. That begins the life of Saul who later becomes Paul the Apostle, a disciple of Jesus Christ.

Now, that situation was a sovereign act of God. That's God doing something outside His Word.

God never promised us that He'd go shine a light around every one of us while we're traveling down the road and tell us to stop doing what we're doing! He doesn't slap everybody whose mad and riding a donkey on the way to hurt someone. No, it was a special incident where God acted sovereignly and did what He wanted to do – to convert Paul the Apostle.

You hear about this kind of thing today with people in foreign places hearing about Jesus and yet, never having missionaries anywhere near them. You also hear about it in strange accidents with people being saved supernaturally from death and that kind of thing. Those are strange occurrences and happen because God acts sovereignly outside of His Word. Why does He do that? I don't know! There are some things we will only know when we get to Heaven!

Wrath, Judgment and Spiritual Law

Some people think God sends hurricanes and other natural disasters to judge His kids and get them to move. While there is a wrathful, judgment side to God, if you are a believer and you obey Him, you'll never see it.

God's wrath isn't reserved for His own children. We're appointed to His grace because of Jesus' blood. God's wrath is for the ungodly and the unrighteous and it comes when the work of sin is finished. Romans 5:9 assures us that, *"Much more then, being now justified by His blood, we shall be saved from wrath through Him."*

There are spiritual laws that can't be broken: *"Then when lust hath conceived, it bringeth forth sin: and sin, when it is finished, bringeth forth death"* (James 1:15). If you sin, and don't accept forgiveness through Jesus' blood, that sin will eventually come to a finished state and death will be waiting. It's sin that destroys a person, not God.

God is like a judge in a courtroom. When a judge looks at a man who's broken the law and he says, "I sentence you to die by lethal injection," does the judge go to jail for sentencing the man? No.

Does the executioner go to jail for putting the drugs in the person? No. Who killed that person? Did the judge kill that person? No. Did the executioner kill that person? No. That is why they can't be charged with murder. What killed the person? The law killed the person.

Sin is a spiritual law. It's what came into the world when man chose to side with satan and reject God's commandment. By man's own free will, he disobeyed God and ushered in satan's sin. That sin, which the Bible calls "iniquity" was born in the heart of satan and brings death. It's a spiritual law that begins with lust, turns to sin, and ends in death.

Does God kill people? No. The sin they choose eventually kills them. All they need to do to escape sin and death is to accept Jesus as Savior. After that, they move out of the path of wrath and into His grace. If they reject Him, their sin will eventually bring about their demise. This is the reason for spreading the Gospel in love to people. It's important that people realize God is good; that He loves them and wants them to live good lives that are free from sin's harsh end.

God will not break His Word, and He will

not choose to sovereignly save people who have chosen to reject Him. He'll protect a person's right to go to hell, if they so choose, just as He will protect their right to go to Heaven. God has given us free will to either choose Him or reject Him, and He will abide by our choice.

Chapter 4
The Lessons of Job,
A Godly and Prosperous Man

If you're talking about sovereignty, you're going to hear about Job! His life is a classic example of misunderstood scripture. You can't blame people. Even Job didn't know what was going on, so his words were littered with confusing ideas about God. I'm going to break this down and share what the story of Job shows me about God in light of the teachings of Jesus about the devil.

The Bible says that Job was a perfect, mature and just man. Why would the devil want to attack Job? Have you ever thought that perhaps it was because Job was not only a perfect, just man but that he was also the richest man in the east? Consider this: if the devil could shut down Job's finances, he could shut down Job's influence in the area. Job was known as a godly man who had prospered.

The devil hates the prosperity of the righteous because it gives them greater influence in the earth. He wanted to wipe Job out, but the devil couldn't even see Job. The Bible says that there was a hedge of protection around him. So, how did he even recognize Job? He recognized him by the blessings.

Satan's Deception, God's Honesty

The devil paid a visit to God. You'll notice that the scripture says he went directly after Job offered burnt offerings for his sons who he thought may have sinned and cursed God in their hearts. The Bible says, one day angelic beings came to present themselves to the Lord and satan came along with them.

When God saw this, He said, *"...Satan, Whence comest thou? Then satan answered the LORD, and said, From going to and fro in the earth, and from walking up and down in it"* (Job 1:7).

Notice that God's first question to the devil is, and I'll paraphrase, 'Where did you just come from, satan?'

Do you think God wasn't aware of where the devil had just come from? Do you think He asked because He was curious? No. God already knew.

When satan answered that he'd just come from walking the earth, it was a deliberately vague and deceitful answer. Of course, we know the devil does roam the earth looking for someone to kill, steal, and destroy, looking for someone to devour. But, I believe God asked him where he'd come from because He already knew that satan had come from somewhere specific – Job's place.

So, God knows satan has come to Him for a reason. He wants information about Job, so God gets right to the point. He says, *"Hast thou considered My servant Job, that there is none like him in the earth, a perfect and an upright man, one that feareth God, and escheweth evil?"* (Job 1:8)

God likes to ask questions like this. This is one of His ways of dealing with deception. Consider Cain and Able. God asks Cain where his brother is, even though He already knows Cain committed murder. It's His way of allowing the person to come clean about his act or motive. He never pounces on a person immediately. God gives them the opportunity to explain themselves. When they don't, He goes straight to the point.

In Cain's case, God talks about his brother. In the devil's case, He talks about Job. You can't pull one over on God. He sees the heart. And, because He's just, He won't withhold truth from anyone, even the devil. He's honest and doesn't bend His just nature to suit the circumstance.

Satan's Critical Words About Job

God was very quick to point out to the devil that Job was a good man who respected Him and refused evil. God compliments Job and even brags on him to the devil. He's proud of Job, and He loves him.

When satan hears this, he is critical and lashes out with this: *"...Doth Job fear God for nought? Hast not Thou made an hedge about him, and about his house, and about all that he hath on every side? Thou hast blessed the work of his hands, and his substance is increased in the land. But put forth Thine hand now, and touch all that he hath, and he will curse Thee to Thy face"* (Job 1:9-11).

Satan saw the blessings and hated Job's love for God. He also hated God's love for Job. That's a point I want you to notice. Even though the devil couldn't *see* Job directly, he came to Heaven with an opinion of Job.

The devil knew Job had a hedge around all his stuff, which means the devil must have been walking around that hedge. He knew about Job's work and his wealth, which means he must have really taken notice of that, and it angered him. He hated to see any of God's children blessed and walking righteously. He was perched and ready to devour Job.

Satan lashes out at God's compliment of Job by saying that Job doesn't love God. He says that if God held Job's material possessions back, Job would curse Him to His face. That was an insult to God, but notice that God doesn't retaliate by withholding information from satan. He tells satan the truth anyway, *"And the LORD said unto satan, Behold, all that he hath is in thy power; only upon himself put not forth thine hand"* (Job 1:12).

God is Truthful and Just, Even with the Devil
Some people think that God *allowed* satan to hurt Job or that God was testing Job. I believe that the truth is that the devil came to God with Job on his mind, looking for ways to hurt him. He wanted information he didn't have. He knew about the hedge and hated Job's goodness and prosperity. He wanted to see Job suffer, and he wanted to know if God would put His hand on

Job and take his stuff away.

Now, God knew that the devil was virtually limitless in hurting mankind. That was the horror of the fall. Sin's admittance into the earth changed everything. Did God *want* to let the devil know this? No. He loved Job and recognized him as a good man. Did He *have* to tell satan his limits? Yes. Because He is a truthful and just God, He did not withhold the information – even though it would hurt Job.

Mankind had given the earth to satan at the fall. At this point, the truth was that satan could touch anything on the earth, and it was very much in his power to inflict harm upon mankind. The devil didn't know this.

The devil told God that if God put *His hand* on Job's stuff to take it away, Job would reject Him. That was ignorance talking.

Did you notice that God didn't agree with the devil about the hand issue? Instead, He said, and I'll paraphrase, 'You can put your hand on everything but Job.' In other words, God was saying that *His* hand wouldn't be the one to take Job's possessions – that was something the devil would stretch out *his* hand to do.

I hope you're getting a revelation on this! This is what I believe with all my heart. There is much to be learned by looking at these old texts in light of Jesus' teaching on the devil and his work within the earth.

The Fear of Job

Now, we know that Job feared greatly because of his kids. He was making those sacrifices for his kids because he was afraid they were cursing God. Maybe they were.

With a wife like Job had, who knows? At Job's lowest point, she was a big ball of discouragement when she said, *"...Dost thou still retain thine integrity? curse God, and die"* (Job 2:9). Now, that's bad! Good thing that he didn't listen! Instead, he told her she was talking like a foolish woman.

In the worst of Job's problems, He said that what he feared the most came upon him (Job 3:25). So, he must have had a lot of fear in his heart and dread in his mind before the devil came to steal, kill, and destroy his life.

Job's Lack of Knowledge

Some people say that Job's story is one of the Bible's oldest and was before Abraham's covenant too. We know he was in another dispensation. It was a different time frame, and we don't know what, if any, covenant there was between God and Job.

The sad part is that Job really didn't know much, if anything, about the devil. He didn't have a revelation of fear and how it negates faith. He didn't realize the devil was the one killing, stealing, and destroying people on earth.

Job just didn't have the knowledge we have today. He believed like most people of his time and background did – that everything good came from God and everything bad came from God. So, his words were littered with this wrong thinking. He was in the dark when it came to the devil, and that lack of knowledge hurt him in a great way.

Other than Ezekiel, Daniel and Isaiah, hardly anybody realized the works of satan in the Old Testament. Those who did were being given words from the Holy Spirit – divine prophecy – that would be understood much later. So, Job was in the dark. You don't hear him rebuking the devil once. You don't see him fighting or even talking about the devil.

Job: He Lacked but He Still Won!

Job didn't have the nine gifts of the Spirit. He didn't have the fruit of the Spirit, against which there is no law. He didn't have the Bible from Genesis to Revelation. He didn't have the Holy Ghost in him. And, if you read the forty-second chapter of Job, he *still* wins in the end and God gives him twice the amount that he lost!

Now, if Job can do that while living in such darkness, how much more can you that have a new covenant through Jesus Christ, the nine gifts, the fruit of the Spirit, revelation knowledge about the devil and the Holy Bible, from Genesis to Revelation, do?

Today, we have everything we need to be a success in this life – spiritually, physically, emotionally and financially. We can't blame God's sovereignty for our lack of success in an area. His will for our lives is good, not bad. It's our job to recognize the devil's mark – stealing, killing, and destroying – and take care of it with the Word.

Chapter 5
When God Gets the Blame

Here's another one people often lay at the feet of God's sovereignty – babies who die. "You know, the reason why the baby died is because God looked into the future and saw that the baby would sin. So, God took the baby out when it was innocent so it would make Heaven its home." I can't tell you how many times I've heard preachers explain the death of a child with this line.

This is an outright false doctrine; it's almost laughable. If it was the case, everybody who ever died and went to hell could holler, "That's not fair!" And, they'd be right. They could say, "Wait a minute, God! Why are You sending me to hell? Why didn't You take me out when I was innocent and pure like You took that baby?"

If God would kill a baby so they won't grow up and go to hell, then He would be an unfair God who cares for one person more than He cares for another. And, the Bible clearly tells us that God is no respecter of persons (Acts 10:34).

Again, the reason that preachers say this, is because they just don't know why the baby died, and they want to offer consolation to those who are grieving. I understand and I realize they just want to show compassion, but lying about God's nature isn't the way to do it. I'd prefer that someone be uncertain about "why" something happened than to be angry with God for something He didn't do.

The Bible tells us that if we lack wisdom in an area, we can ask for it from God, and He will give it liberally (James 1:5). In these situations, I suggest the grieving parents really get alone with God and allow Him to minister to their heart one-on-one. Peace is found in the presence of God. Wisdom is found in the presence of God. It's the only thing that can heal a person's heart from such tragedy. To lie to a person who is going through such a tragedy is wrong. It just puts a wedge between them and God – a wedge of anger for the loss.

Satan kills. God gives life. The comfort is in knowing that God doesn't lose one of them. Every child who ever died on earth, went to Heaven and began growing up there. Some people don't believe that, but I know it's true because I've been there, and I've seen the children with my own eyes. It doesn't matter if a baby dies after five years on earth or only two days after conception, that life lives on in Heaven. What a childhood! To be raised in Heaven learning the oracles of God – free from sin, sickness and pain.

You can't kill a baby and you can't kill a Christian. They come back. People that you know who have died of cancer, diabetes, high blood pressure, accidents or some other tragedy are coming back and one day they're going to look that lying devil in the eyes and say, "What? This? This is what caused all the trouble in the world? Boy, you killed me once, but you can't kill me twice! I am back here again, glory to God, with a redeemed, glorified body, and I'm going to cheer when God kicks you into the fire!" We will see that happen.

As Christians, it's our job to stand with people in faith, and if we don't know something, then we ought to have the integrity to say it. We ought to have the guts to say, "Look, I don't know what happened, but I know God loves you and wouldn't hurt you. We are going to pray together and search this thing out in the wisdom and power of God. God is going to give you wisdom concerning this situation and peace for your mind."

We all have an appointed time to die and after this comes the judgment of God, according to Hebrews 9:27. Sometimes, the devil steals a life before its appointed time, but we all have a time to die. It's important that we do what we can to keep the appointment and don't show up earlier than we should!

Sometimes in life people want to go earlier. Did you know Paul the Apostle was trying to die for years before he was supposed to? He talked to God about it, begging Him to get him out of here. But he ended up saying that for your sake, it was better for him to stay. He knew the Lord had a destiny for him to fulfill, even though he wanted to go home to Heaven. God called Paul to the Gentiles and he couldn't leave until that foundation of truth was laid plain for the Gentile people.

That's why when he was on death row, he didn't bawl and squall about dying. Instead Paul said, and I'll paraphrase, 'Give me a piece of paper. I am going to write down one more revelation before I go home to be with God.' He was still taking care of his body because he said, 'Give me a coat.' He was still taking care of his mind because he said, 'Give me some books.' But He was taking care of his destiny by saying, 'But, give me the parchments. Let me tell you more about what God has said.' He understood that before his appointment with death, he had to fulfill his destiny. That's a man of faith.

Temptations, Tests and Trials

Here's another one that God always gets the blame for – life's tough circumstances. But, did Jesus *ever* tell us His Father was going to send us through temptations, tests and trials to teach us something? No. He said in Matthew 26:41, *"Watch and pray, that ye enter not into temptation: the spirit indeed is willing, but the flesh is weak."*

Would Jesus tell you to watch and pray not to enter into temptation if He knew it was His own Dad who was sending them? Come on! Not when He later rebukes the devil for tempting Him! The devil is the tempter. Jesus just knew our flesh was weak and the devil would prey upon that. So, He told us to pray about it.

Then, why did Peter say we should count our trials as precious as gold? Because he knew that going through a trial is tough, but it shows you where you are...and besides, Peter went through the toughest trial of his life when Jesus was taken captive. He fell and betrayed Christ just like Judas did. The difference was that Judas didn't accept forgiveness, but Peter did.

Peter knew that trials prove your loyalty, and once he had missed the mark and then accepted forgiveness, he realized that he could defeat anything the devil threw at him. He'd been through the worst of it and had survived because of God's grace. Not only did he survive, he became like the rock that Jesus' church was built upon! And Matthew 16:18 says the gates of hell would never prevail against that church!

That shows you that even when you fall, if you ask for forgiveness, God can raise you up and use you in a great way. Judas lost out because he couldn't receive grace. Peter went on to do great things for God simply because he received forgiveness and wouldn't let the devil beat him up for his entire life for betraying Jesus. The devil brings condemnation, heaping criticism on people. God gives grace and forgiveness, and He never brings those old things up again.

The spirit of people who walk in faith is different from those who walk in doubt. After Peter received forgiveness, he was back on track. In Acts three, when Peter, James and John saw the crippled man at the gate called "Beautiful" they didn't give that crippled man sympathy. They gave him compassion like Jesus did. They said, *"Silver and gold have I none; but such as I have give I thee: In the name of Jesus Christ of Nazareth rise up and walk. And he took him by the right hand, and lifted him up: and immediately his feet and ankle bones received strength"* (Acts 3:6-7).

Notice that they didn't wait for the man to get up, they reached down and grabbed him. Why? Because they believed it was going to happen. And notice this. They didn't even say, 'Look on Jesus' before the miracle happened. Verse four says, *"And Peter, fastening his eyes upon him with John, said, Look on us"* (Acts 3:4). Wouldn't that shake up religious people if preachers went around saying that today?

No, Peter and John knew God would get the

glory regardless and they wanted the man to look directly at them and know that they didn't have silver and gold to drop in his cup, but what they did have, they would freely give him. What they did have was the power of God working in their lives. In the very next chapter, however, you'll notice that God poured out His great grace upon them and they had more than silver and gold laid at their feet!

Acts 4:33-35 says, *"And with great power gave the apostles witness of the resurrection of the Lord Jesus: and great grace was upon them all. Neither was there any among them that lacked: for as many as were possessors of lands or houses sold them, and brought the prices of the things that were sold, And laid them down at the apostles' feet: and distribution was made unto every man according as he had need."*

God's grace was sufficient for the apostles of Jesus. Every need was met so they could do the work that God had called them to do.

Chapter 6
Jesus, the Light of the World

Jesus didn't go around denying sickness, disease and problems. However, He denied their right to remain in a person of faith. He told us that there would be obstacles in life. Tribulation is part of life in a sin-filled earth – it's as simple as that. There is a war going on, and sometimes, the devil wins a battle or two.

Does it mean it is God's will if the devil wins in one of his attempts at killing, stealing, and destroying one of God's kids? No. It just means that some way, some how, he got a punch in. But his day is coming. We are going to win this war against the devil and all his demons. God tells us so at the end of the Bible. The idiot is going to burn.

Jesus taught us to be of good cheer when tribulations come. Why? Because He has overcome the world with His sacrifice and you have a covenant that God won't break.

Through Jesus' example, we learn how to live. Through His teachings, we learn how to think right – to banish all the dark, ignorant thinking, and start understanding what it means to live clean in a sin-filled earth. Through His death, we gain the power and authority we need to destroy the works of the devil.

That authority is for exposing the devil's work in your life and the life of your loved ones. It's for rebuking, resisting, and watching the devil flee. It's for saving the lost and healing the sick. It's for overcoming everything satan throws in your path.

What I'm trying to get across to you in this book is simple. God is good. He loves you and cared enough about your life that He sent Jesus to show you some things, to open your eyes, and to shine a light on the dark thinking of yesteryear.

When you are weak, God says you're strong (2 Cor. 12:10). How can He say that? Because greater is He who lives in you, than he who is running loose in this world (1 John 4:4).

If God be for you, who can be against you? (Rom. 8:31). And if you say to that mountain in your life, "Be gone," and you believe it and don't doubt in your heart, it's going to start on its descent into the sea. Those problems, regardless of their size, are going to start going down (Mark 11:23).

God will be glorified by your faith; by the miracles that happen when you use His Word to overcome the devil's plans for your destruction. You already know that he's got three things in his job description – stealing, killing, and destroying (John 10:10). Now that you know, take a hard look at your life and the circumstances surrounding it. Any stealing going on? Any destroying? How about killing? That's his mark.

Your covenant with God was made with the innocent blood of Jesus, and if you think He's going to dismiss that just because He's sovereign, somebody has sold you a lie. God loves you, and He loves His Son. He is sovereign alright... outside of His Word.

God's Word is His will and you can count on Him to support it. If He said it, you can count on it. God has promised to keep His covenant with you!

"My covenant will I not break,
nor alter the thing that is gone out of My lips."
Psalm 89:34

Look for these other books by
Jesse Duplantis

The Everyday Visionary

The Ministry of Cheerfulness
Also available in Braille

Heaven: Close Encounters of the God Kind
Also available in Braille or Spanish

God Is Not Enough, He's Too Much!
Also available in Braille

Breaking the Power of Natural Law
Also available in Braille

Jambalaya for the Soul
Also available in Braille

Wanting A God You Can Talk To
Also available in Braille

What In Hell Do You Want?

JDM Mini-books

Don't Be Affected by the World's Message

The Battle of Life

Running Toward Your Giant

Keep Your Foot on the Devil's Neck

One More Night With the Frogs

Leave It in the Hands of a Specialist

Keeping a Clean Heart

Understanding Salvation
Also available in Spanish

JESSE DUPLANTIS MINISTRIES
Preaching the Gospel to the World